# Speke Hall

A guide to its history and owners

A. J. Tibbles

Merseyside County Museums

# Foreword

**Foreword by Lord Gibson**
**Chairman, the National Trust**

The publication of this new guidebook marks the near completion of a major programme of repairs to the building. I am delighted to have been given this opportunity to express, on behalf of the National Trust, our gratitude to Merseyside County Council who have managed and promoted Speke Hall with such distinction since 1974. Great credit is due to them for having undertaken the work under their lease with much perseverance over a number of years, with the generous assistance of the Historic Buildings Council. I can congratulate the County Council on the tremendous progress that has been made. Further, I am happy to say excellent relations exist between the National Trust and the County Council, which augurs well for the future of the Hall, now in a sounder condition than at any time in the last 300 years.

*Gibson*

**Foreword by Councillor Jim Riley**
**Chairman Arts and Culture Committee**
**Merseyside County Council**

I am delighted to welcome the publication of this new guidebook to Speke Hall. The Merseyside County Council when they assumed responsibility for Speke Hall in 1974 recognised that this building is of truly national significance and they also realised that drastic action was required to save the building from severe decay inflicted by the ravages of time. Despite the severe economic situation and with the outstanding support and financial assistance of the Historic Buildings Council, under the Chairmanship of Mrs. Jennifer Jenkins, major structural repairs and restoration have been carried out over the last seven years. As a result of these efforts the future of Speke Hall is safeguarded for the people of Merseyside and those from elsewhere who wish to visit and enjoy this beautiful building. Lastly may I say how encouraged we are by the confidence and support expressed by Lord Gibson and the National Trust for the County Council's efforts in restoring and managing Speke Hall.

*Jim Riley*

# Speke Hall

Speke Hall is one of a number of large timber-framed manor houses in the north-west of England built in the medieval and Tudor periods, only a handful of which survive in their original state today. It was built during the period from the late 15th to the early 17th centuries by members of the Norris family who were important landowners in South Lancashire and Cheshire. Remarkably there have been no major alterations or additions to the structure and the building is an unusually fine example of a Tudor gentry family's manor house. The Hall remained the main Norris residence until the estate passed by marriage to the Beauclerk family in the mid 18th century. The Beauclerks took little interest in the house and a period of neglect followed. In 1795 the house and estate were bought by Richard Watt, a self-made Liverpool merchant. Although some interior restoration work was carried out in the early 19th century, the Watts did not, in fact, live at Speke for most of the first half of the century.

In about 1855 Richard Watt, the last of five members of the family to bear that name, took up residence at Speke, carrying out further restoration work to the interior and re-furnishing the house throughout. After Richard Watt's death in 1865 this work was continued by his daughter, Adelaide, and also by F. R. Leyland, the shipping magnate and patron of the arts, who leased the house during her childhood. It is the home they created which we see today.

Miss Watt died in 1921. After a period in the hands of Trustees, the house and grounds were accepted by the National Trust in 1943. They are now administered by Merseyside County Council.

The North Front

The South Front

# The history of Speke Hall

Speke is first mentioned in the Domesday Book of 1086. This records that, at the time of the Norman Conquest, the manor of Speke had been held by a Saxon lord, Uctred, who was then the largest landowner in Lancashire. It consisted of two carucates of land (perhaps 200–300 acres) and was valued at 64 pence. By 1086 the manor had been given to Count Roger of Poitou, one of the supporters of William the Conqueror.

For the next few hundred years the issue of ownership is complicated. The feudal system was a complex arrangement of land tenure. Theoretically all land belonged to the King. In practice land was granted by him to tenants-in-chief, who in turn granted tenures and sub-tenures. By 1170 Speke was included in the Master Forestership of Lancashire, though actual tenure was in the hands of the Molyneux family, who were to retain nominal overlordship until the late 16th century.

In the early 13th century the manor was divided into two parts, with one half being granted to Sir Patrick de Haselwell and the other half to Robert Erneys of Chester. Sir Patrick had two daughters who married brothers, Alan and John le Noreis. By 1317 John le Noreis was in sole possession of the full Haselwell half of the manor and from 1332 he leased the Erneys land. John and his wife, Nicola, had a house at Speke by 1314, and from them descended a line of Norrises who were to live at Speke until the 18th century. The two halves of the manor were finally united in Norris ownership when Sir Henry Norris married Alice Erneys in about 1390.

During the course of the 14th and 15th centuries the Norrises established themselves as leading members of the local gentry. They built up extensive estates, as the rental of Thomas Norris of about 1468 records, owning land in many areas of what is now Liverpool, around Chester, on the Wirral and even as far away as Anglesey. Little is known of their house at this time. It is likely to have been a timber-framed building on the same site but on a much smaller scale than the present house. It probably consisted of a hall, with a cross-wing for the family's private accommodation at one end and a kitchen and service wing at the other end. Possibly the Kitchen was a separate structure.

Towards the end of the 15th century the Norrises began to rebuild the house and over the next hundred years or so, the Speke Hall that we know today was erected. It was at this period that the Norrises were at the height of their wealth and influence. Building work probably began in the time of Sir William Norris (d.1506) who inherited the estate in about 1490. He was succeeded by his son, Henry, who fought at the battle of Flodden, under the command of Sir William Molyneux, his nominal overlord. Henry died in 1524, and along with his wife Clemence, is commemorated in a brass in Childwall Church. His son, Sir William, was a particularly active member of the community who held a number of local positions, culminating in a term as Mayor of Liverpool in 1554–55. He took part in several military campaigns, including the Sack of Edinburgh in 1544, when on his own admission he stole several books from the Royal Library. He also fought at the battle of Musselborough when he captured the standard of Bothwell of Balmuto. It was at this last battle, however, that his eldest son was killed. Sir William married twice and his large family of nineteen children may partially explain the scale of building at this time. This included the erection of the Great Parlour and western ranges, and the re-modelling of the eastern range. He appears to have been a scholarly man and showed considerable interest in the history of his family. He annotated many family deeds and in 1564 compiled the 'Genealogical Declaration', which contains details of many of the early Norrises.

Sir William died in 1568 and was succeeded by Edward, his third son, who built the northern and final range of the house. The years of Edward Norris's tenure of the manor saw the beginning of a difficult period for the family. From the 1530s the religious upheavals of the Reformation had seen the advantage oscillate between the Protestants and the Catholics, but the accession of Elizabeth I in 1558 saw the virtual victory of Protestantism in England. Increasingly Catholics were viewed with suspicion. After Elizabeth's excommunication in 1570 and the declared aim of other Catholic monarchs to overthrow her, English Catholics were seen as subversives and possible traitors. The Norrises, like many of their neighbours, clung to the old faith and found themselves gradually alienated from the Establishment. Priests were frequently sheltered at Speke, as in 1598 when it was reported that 'Little Sir Richard' and 'Sir Peter' 'for the most parte lodged in a chamber over the parlour.' A number of priest holes were also built into the house.

In general Edward Norris seems to have maintained

a low profile and conformed in many respects, but his son, Sir William, who succeeded him in 1606, was a totally different character. He was reckless and incautious, making no secret of his religious allegiance. In 1626 he was accused of sending arms and money 'to the king's enemies beyond the seas.' The combination of heavy recusancy fines and his own financial mismanagement, brought the family to the edge of financial ruin. He was forced to sell some of his estates and Speke itself was mortgaged to raise funds. Just before his death in 1630, he was involved in an incident over church attendance at Childwall Church when he drew his sword on Edward More, the investigating magistrate. This resulted in a summons before the Court of Star Chamber and a fine of £1,000. The fine was later commuted to £250 but his son, William (d.1651) was left in dire financial straits. This was further compounded after the Civil War, when having supported the Royalist cause, the Norris estates were confiscated by Parliament.

Henry and Clemence Norris, from their brasses in Childwall Church

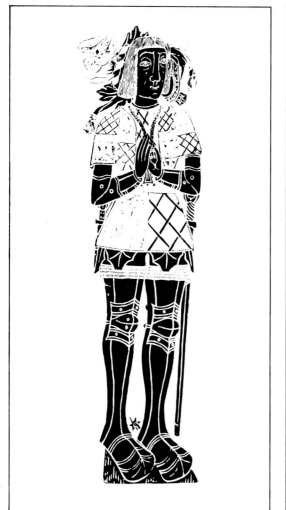

Thomas Norris, who succeeded at this low ebb in 1651, appears to be the first member of the family to embrace Anglicanism. Gradually he was able to rebuild the family fortunes. The Speke estate was recovered after the Restoration of the Monarchy in 1660 and members of the family began to hold public office again after a break of nearly a century. Thomas had seven sons, four of whom were to hold Speke after his death in about 1687. They were all figures of some importance, contributing to both local and national affairs. The eldest, Thomas (d.1700), was involved in the political and business activities of Liverpool, serving on the Common Council, as an MP and as Sheriff of Lancashire. Sir William (d.1702) was also an MP, but is best remembered for his mission to India as Ambassador to the Great Mogul. Edward Norris (d.1726), a doctor of medicine, was also MP for Liverpool from 1714 to 1722. The youngest brother, Richard, was a merchant, much involved with the West Indies trade, including the slave trade. He was a leading political figure in Liverpool and as MP in 1708–9 was partially responsible for obtaining the Act which allowed the town to build its first dock. None of these brothers had a male heir and on Richard's death in

The North Entrance

Adelaide Watt (1857–1921)

1731 the estate passed to Thomas's daughter, Mary. In 1736 Mary Norris married Lord Sidney Beauclerk (pronounced Beau-clare), fifth son of the Duke of St Albans, a rather rakish figure known to his contemporaries as 'Worthless Sidney'. Mary Norris's strong attachment to her ancestral home was not shared by her husband, or by her son, Topham, who was asked to adopt his mother's maiden name. After her death in 1766 the house seems to have been let to tenants. Topham did, however, commission a Survey of the estate in 1774 which provides much useful information and also features the earliest representation of the Hall. Charles George Beauclerk who succeeded him in 1781 paid equally little attention to Speke and considerable damage was done to the fabric and contents of the Hall by various tenants.

In 1795 the estate was sold for £73,500 to Richard Watt, a Liverpool merchant. Watt was born of humble origins in 1724 at Standish, near Wigan. Tradition maintains that as a young man he drove the first hired carriage in Liverpool before going to seek his fortune in the West Indies. By the time of his death he had a plantation in Jamaica and a flourishing mercantile business with offices and warehouses in Liverpool's dockland. Richard Watt died within twelve months of buying Speke and never seems to have actually lived in the house. His heir and nephew, also named Richard Watt, lived in Yorkshire, at Bishop Burton, near Beverley, where he continued to reside. Some restoration work was undertaken in the Great Hall about 1811–12 and several rooms were refurnished at that time. However, any plans for the family to use Speke disappeared on Richard Watt's death in mid 1812 and the new furniture was all sold by auction.

The third Richard Watt (d.1855) lived at Bishop Burton throughout his life and from at least 1840 Speke was rented to Joseph Brereton, a local timber merchant. The Hall was badly neglected at this time and caused one writer to quote it as 'grievous proof of the want of taste and right feeling of the present owner.'

On Watt's death in 1855, Speke was inherited by his grandson, the fifth and last Richard Watt. He seems to have had strong local connections, having been born at Speke and educated in Liverpool, and it was under him that the Hall saw a revival. He came to live at Speke and for the first time in over a hundred years the house was lived in as a family home. He carried out further restoration work, particularly in the Great Parlour, and was responsible for completely refurnishing the Hall. The furniture was specially chosen to complement the building and consisted of heavily carved and stained oak pieces, drawing their inspiration from the furniture and styles of the 16th and 17th centuries. He was also responsible for laying out the garden and grounds which immediately surround the Hall.

Richard Watt died unexpectedly in 1865 at the tragically young age of 30, leaving his eight-year-old daughter, Adelaide, an orphan. She was brought up in Scotland by her guardian and great-uncle, James Sprot, and the house was again leased. This time the tenant was F. R. Leyland, the shipping magnate and noted patron of the arts. He appreciated Speke and was responsible for carrying our further work in the ground floor rooms on the west and north-west sides of the house. It was in his time that James McNeill Whistler, the painter, was a frequent house guest.

In 1878 Adelaide Watt came of age and Leyland moved to nearby Woolton Hall. Although absent from Speke for long periods, it was her principal residence and she took a meticulous interest in all that went on in the house and on the estate, as her letters to Mr Graves, her agent, testify. She was consulted on the design of new buildings, repairs to farm properties, the ordering of materials, the livestock of the Home Farm, the activities of the townspeople or such matters as the type of tiles to be used in the drains or the conduct of the local police constable. Her tenants and servants were expected to be 'sober, honest and industrious', attend the Church of England and vote Conservative. She was eager to see that the Hall was properly maintained and took a close personal interest in all the repair work, stipulating materials to be used and firms to be employed.

Miss Watt never married and on her death in 1921 the house was left in trust for her cousin and various members of the Norris family with whom she was in contact. However, by an alternative clause in her will the Hall was offered to the National Trust in 1942 and accepted in 1943. In the following year the Hall and grounds were leased to the Liverpool City Council. Following local government reorganisation in 1974 Merseyside County Council took on the tenancy and has since had administrative and financial responsibility for the property.

Building of the present Speke Hall probably began towards the end of the 15th century and continued for a period of about 100 years. It was a piecemeal process of gradual addition and replacement, and parts of the old house survived for a considerable time after building began. Indeed it is likely that some parts of the former building were incorporated in the present structure and certainly there is evidence that some of the timber was re-used. Initially there was no formal plan and the building developed as needs dictated, though perhaps using former foundations in some places. Each of the four ranges is different on its external front, though in the late 16th century some degree of symmetry and uniformity of decoration was created on the courtyard facades.

The construction of the house is typical of timber-framed buildings of the period. The oak frame rests on a base of red sandstone. It is a box-like structure consisting of base plates, main wall posts, wall plates, and tie beams. These main members are stiffened with smaller, intermediate timbers and the walls are infilled with wattle and daub. This is formed by small staves of oak which are interlaced in a basket-like fashion with hazel twigs and then covered with daub, made up of marl, cow dung and chopped straw. It is usually finished with a top coat of lime plaster.

9

Above the main frame is the roof, formed by principal rafters, purlins, common rafters and the ridge. The roof cover is of sandstone slabs.

The majority of timbers are held together by mortise and tenon joints, though more complicated scarf and lap joints are also found. All the joints are secured by oak pegs. Much of the timber-work is not structural, although it has a strengthening effect. It was included mainly for decorative purposes. This is true of the diagonal timbering of the north and south fronts and the quatrefoil panels which are found on the two main facades and on the courtyard walls. This type of timberwork, and in such quantity, is particularly characteristic of timber-framed houses of Lancashire and Cheshire.

Nearly all timber-framed buildings were prefabricated. All the joints were pre-cut and the main timbers were assembled on the ground before erection, often in a carpenter's yard. The timbers were then marked with Roman numerals so that they could be put up exactly as they had been prepared on the ground.

A Bay in the Courtyard

Carpenters' Mark in the West Range Roof

It is most unlikely that the timbers were originally painted and the stark 'black and white' effect probably only dates from the last century. The timbers were allowed to weather naturally and the limewash was less brilliant than today because of impurities.

The first substantial part of the Hall to be built was the Great Hall. This was probably erected c.1490–1506, though it is possibly of a later date. Parts of the former house were almost certainly left standing at this time and it is likely that there were cross-wings at either end of the Great Hall. It is also possible that the south bay was part of the earlier building incorporated within the new structure.

The next major addition was the Great Parlour wing, which probably dates from c.1525–35. The north bay of the Great Hall was added at about the same time.

The period from about 1540 to 1570 probably saw substantial changes to the house. The west range, with further family rooms, was added, the south-east wing was altered and extended and the east range was re-modelled. At some point in the late 16th century the courtyard facade of the south range was altered on the eastern side to create a bay to balance the Great Hall bay and a large false window completed the symmetrical appearance of this side of the courtyard.

The last major addition was the building of the north range, which an inscription over the main entrance records was completed by Edward Norris in 1598. Two minor additions in the early 17th century were a sandstone gate to the garden in 1605 and a porch from the Great Parlour in 1612.

A dairy and laundry were added to the building in the area adjoining the Kitchen courtyard about 1860. The laundry was altered and extended in the early 1950s and is now used as a tearoom.

In 1977 a comprehensive programme of repairs was begun following a full survey on the condition of the fabric. It was found that substantial parts of the building were in need of urgent attention if Speke Hall was to survive in its present form. A combination of factors was to blame, including wet rot, attack by death-watch beetle and other wood boring insects, a deteriorating roof cover, together with a number of serious structural problems. The repair programme has been financed by Merseyside County Council, with substantial grants from the Historic Buildings Council of England.

c 1490–1506

c 1525–1535

c 1540–1570

c 1570–1598

19th Century

# The Interior

**The Courtyard**   The cobbled courtyard is dominated by two yew trees, known locally as Adam and Eve, which are reputed to be older than any existing part of the Hall. On entering the courtyard the main family rooms lie to the right and the service rooms and domestic accommodation are on the left. Throughout most of its history, visitors would have entered the house by crossing the courtyard and going through the Screens Passage into the Great Hall.

**The Great Hall**   When it was originally built at the beginning of the 16th century, the Great Hall was considerably different from its present appearance. There was no compass bay on the courtyard side and there were windows at the upper level only. The walls consisted of the timber-framing and plain plaster infill panels, though the main wall posts were heavily moulded to match the ceiling beams. There is some evidence that tapestries or painted cloths were hung on the walls. Because of the arrangement of the ceiling beams, it might appear that the chimney-breast and fireplace are a later addition, but this is unlikely to be so.

The decoration of the chimney-breast is unusual and is executed in a rather crude late Gothic style. It is completed in plaster and consists of varying motifs including quatrefoils, crenellations, ogee and trefoil headed arches, and a series of heads, traditionally

The Courtyard

**12** ✥ said to represent Sir William Norris (d.1568) and his family. The oak mantelbeam is carved with a cable and vine decoration and immediately above this there was originally a band of herringbone brickwork, plastered over since the early 19th century.

The oak panelling was erected in 1564, according to a former inscription. Most impressive is 'The Great Wainscot' at the western end, with its fine pilasters and carved heads in early Flemish Renaissance style. The busts, which are of oak and plaster, represent Roman Emperors, except for the two in the bottom left-hand corner which are in contemporary dress of the mid 16th century and are probably portraits of the patron, who commissioned the panelling, and his wife. The panelling does not seem to have been made for Speke but was adapted to the room. One suggestion is that it came via the Smallwood family, whose daughter Edward Norris married, and who had strong trading links with the Low Countries. The carved panel over the door bears the arms of Edward Norris.

In the late 18th century the Great Hall was maltreated and the panelling was 'much broken and defaced.' The panels and many of the busts on 'The Great Wainscot' were repaired when the Great Hall was restored in about 1811–12. The work was directed by George Bullock, the noted furniture

The Great Hall and 'Great Wainscot'

The Great Hall

The Great Parlour

maker and designer, who may have provided the furniture, which was 'designed after much study and attention to suit the Antique Costume of true Baronial Magnificence.' Sadly none of this furniture has survived.

Contrary to popular belief, it is most unlikely that the Norris family ever lived and ate communally with their servants and retainers in the Great Hall. For occasional feasts and celebrations they may have dined in state under 'The Great Wainscot', but on an everyday basis they would have used one of their more intimate rooms, probably the Little Parlour. The Great Hall was intended to impress the visitor and, by its size and grandeur, to reflect the social standing of the family. Even in the last century it was little used and though F. R. Leyland was initially reported to want 'always to dine in the Hall' the attempt was soon abandoned 'as the wind *howls* rather dismally.'

The furniture mostly dates from the second half of the 17th century. It is made of oak and is carved with a variety of motifs including flower heads, lozenges, lunettes, scrolls and other geometrical patterns. Many of the items were acquired by the Watts, but were distributed throughout the house. They have been brought together in the Great Hall to create a little of the atmosphere of the Norris period, which is so submerged elsewhere in the house.

The large portrait in the bay is of John Middleton, 'The Child of Hale', a local giant reputedly 9' 2" tall, who was taken to the court of King James I.

**The Great Parlour** The Great Parlour was constructed in the early 16th century, c.1524–35. It was built as part of a wing to provide more spacious accommodation for family use and was always intended as one of the most important rooms in the house.

The appearance of the Parlour when first built was probably simpler than now with several of its most attractive features, such as the ceiling, bay window and overmantel, being added in the course of the following century. It is likely to have been panelled and there is evidence that the ceiling was of oak boards laid to give a checkerboard effect.

The Genealogical Overmantel was carved about 1560 and features three generations of the Norris family who were mainly responsible for building the Hall. To the left is Henry Norris, his wife and their five children. In the centre Sir William sits at a table flanked by his two wives and accompanied by all

nineteen of his children. There is a symbolic reference to his eldest son who was killed at the battle of Musselborough in 1547, in the naked prostrate figure with skull and bones in the lower left panel. Sir William's second son, who also predeceased him, may be portrayed by the naked figure in the adjoining panel. In the right-hand panel is Edward Norris with his wife, Margaret, and two of their children. Although the carving shows Flemish influence in the decoration, it is noticeably more naive than 'The Great Wainscot' and is almost certainly of English workmanship.

The principal feature of the interior is the early Jacobean ceiling of c.1600–10. Stucco decoration was a technique imported from Italy and became popular in the Elizabethan period. The ceiling is divided into 15 square panels, each of which is decorated with one of five designs – pomegranates, roses, lilies, grapes or hazelnuts. The beams have designs of trailing hops and honeysuckle.

The bay overlooking the west moat was added in the late 16th century and its stucco ceiling features a classical figure and scrollwork.

The Great Parlour was kept mainly for entertaining and formal use rather than the everyday needs of the family. Certainly its furnishings in 1624 with an extending long table and cupboards covered with green cloths and the stools and chairs upholstered in green silk with fringes, suggest sumptuous formality rather than intimacy.

The Parlour suffered particularly in the late 18th and early 19th centuries when there are records of an inlaid floor being used for firewood and in 1848 a visitor commented that it had been 'grievously neglected' with windows boarded up, panelling crumbling and ivy forcing its way in. The situation was rectified in the following decade by the work of Richard Watt and this is very forcibly reflected in its present appearance. The furniture dates from this period and mostly consists of the heavily carved and stained oak that is so typical of Speke. Of particular note is the large sideboard which is in the style of the Warwick School of Carvers and similar to the famous Charlecote Buffet, shown at the Great Exhibition in 1851. It incorporates a late 16th century carved relief panel, which features scenes from the Old Testament book of Esther.

**The Blue Drawing Room** This was probably the Little Parlour of the early inventories and was the room commonly used by the Norris family, as its contents in 1624 make clear. Apart from the three tables, plate cupboard and stools, all either upholstered in blue or covered with blue cloths, there were a number of more personal items. These included a 'mapp contayning the descripcon of Jherusalem with a Latin book belonging to yt' (the only book mentioned in the house), a 'great callendar hanging on the wall', a toasting fork and a 'tosting iron for cakes'. There were also three 'payre of playing tables' (backgammon boards) and 'one chesse boord & chesse men with a lether bagg to putt them in'.

Little is known of the appearance of the room at this time, though recently it has been discovered that the walls were once wood grained, i.e. painted to resemble panelling. This may date to the late 17th century and possibly ties up with an account of c.1685 for 'penting of Mr Norrises Little Parler'. The room was fully redecorated in the mid 1850s when the present suite of furniture was acquired. It is made of tulipwood and rosewood with ormolu mounts and copies the French Rococo style. Over the years a number of different wallpapers have been hung, but the use of the William Morris 'Willow' pattern dates back to about 1935. This was replaced in March 1981 by the present paper which is an exact copy of the Morris paper, printed from the original blocks.

**The Northern and Western Ground Floor Rooms** Very little is known about these rooms prior

The Great Parlour

The Blue Drawing Room

William Morris Wallpaper, 'Trellis' design, in the Corridors

William Morris Wallpaper, 'Pomegranate' design, in the Library

to the last century. The Morning Room may have been 'the schoole chamber' in 1624 and one of the rooms in the west range was probably a chapel in the 16th century. By 1848 the west range was 'a complete wreck' and there is evidence that part of this range was being used as a kitchen and scullery by the tenant.

Although the Morning Room served as a dining room for Richard Watt, the rooms in the west range were little used until 1867–68 when F. R. Leyland restored them for use as a Billiard Room, Library, Gun Room and Cloakroom. He was responsible for installing the panelling, doors and carving and it was

he who originally had the William Morris wallpapers hung. All three of Morris's earliest designs were used, 'Trellis' in the corridors, and 'Daisy' and 'Pomegranate' in the Library and Gun Room. The furniture and furnishings are mostly those acquired by Richard and Adelaide Watt.

**The Kitchen** Although this wing of the house probably dates from the mid 16th century, the kitchen incorporates part of an earlier structure. In the alcove is a sandstone wall with round-headed windows which may date from the 15th century. It is perhaps a survival of an earlier separate kitchen on this site. The unusually high windows on the

The Morning Room

courtyard side were to prevent servants being distracted from their duties.

Originally cooking was done over an open fire but this was blocked up when a close range was installed in the mid-Victorian period. The present range dates from about 1910. The other equipment in the Kitchen and in the two former larders was in constant use until Miss Watt's death in 1921.

**The Servants' Hall**   This room is on the site of the family chapel, which was built in 1598 as part of the north range. This can be confirmed by the arched window now only visible from outside. It probably fell into disuse in the 17th century and in the 19th century was used first as a Laundry and then as a

Servants' Hall. Outside in the corridor is a series of bells used to summon servants to the appropriate room.

**The Bedrooms**   The main family bedrooms are on the first floor of the north and west ranges of the building. Those normally on view include the Blue Bedroom, the Green Bedroom, the Royal Bedroom and the Tapestry Room. Each has an accompanying dressing room.

The Blue and Green Bedrooms are named after the colour of their furnishings in Miss Watt's time. The Royal Bedroom is so-called because of an unsubstantiated tradition that Charles I slept in the room in 1630. It made enough impression for the

The Kitchen Alcove

Watts to obtain the engravings of Charles I, Henrietta Maria and their children, which still hang there. The Tapestry Room has borne that name since 1700, though at that time it contained more tapestries than now.

Most of the present furniture in the bedrooms dates from the refurnishing of Richard Watt. None of the beds are original 16th or 17th century pieces, but were made up in the 1850s of some genuine woodwork and some contemporary work, carved and stained to blend with the old. For instance, the bed in the Blue Bedroom incorporates a 17th century carving of the Last Supper in the footboard and other 17th century carved figures in the headboard. Many of the other pieces are Victorian but use decorative motifs of the 16th and 17th centuries, and in particular draw on the style of the Flemish Renaissance.

The tapestries are 17th century Flemish – two feature scenes from the story of Jupiter, and others are part of a series of the Four Elements.

This part of the building houses several reminders of the period when Catholic priests used the house as a refuge. In the Blue Bedroom is a spyhole giving a view of the main approach to the house. There are also hiding places in spaces alongside the chimneys in the Green and Tapestry Bedrooms.

The Tapestry Room is also known as the 'haunted room' and a ghost has been associated with Speke since the middle of the last century.

The Royal Bedroom, c.1907

'Bird's Eye View' by Frederick Thorpe, 1907

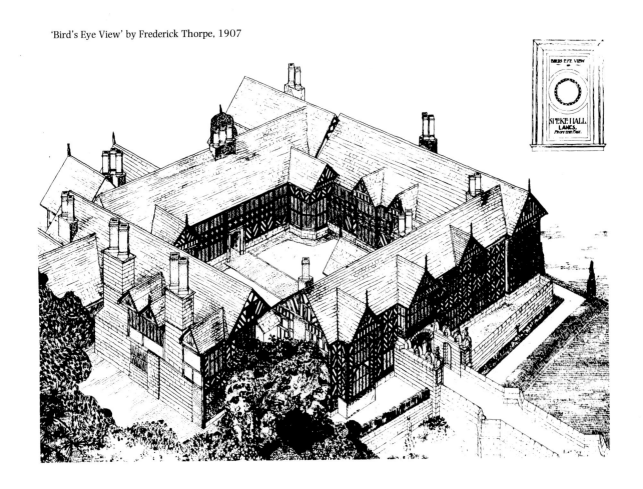

# Gardens and moat

The site of Speke Hall has almost certainly been moated since medieval times, when it was presumably surrounded on all four sides. The earliest reference to the moat is in 1693 when it was stocked with carp and perch, a reminder that from the earliest times moats were important as sources of fresh fish. The 1781 survey map shows the moat water-filled on the eastern and north-eastern sides but the area to the west appears to be dry. By the mid 19th century the whole of the moat seems to have been drained.

It is likely that there was a garden near the house from at least the Tudor period and in 1624 gardeners were employed at Speke. An account book of 1710–19 indicates a considerable amount of activity in the gardens at this time. For instance, in 1711 there is reference to 'weeding in Garden Courts', 'mowing ye squares' and 'dressing ye squares when mowed'. There were also kitchen gardens for soft fruits and vegetables and some items were grown under glass in the 'Gardiners hott bed glasses'. A variety of fruit trees were grown in the orchards.

The South Front. c.1865

The first evidence for the layout of the grounds comes from the 1781 Survey. This shows the area to the north of the house as 'The Green' and to the south-east was a formal garden, orchards and a hopyard. It seems likely that the gardens were subject to the same neglect as the house in the late 18th and early 19th centuries and a number of views of the period show a fairly open aspect in the immediate vicinity of the Hall.

The whole garden area was redesigned for the last Richard Watt between 1855 and 1865, when the present basic layout of lawns, borders, paths and hedges was established. There was extensive planting of rhododendrons and azaleas, and yew was widely used for hedging. No substantial changes have been made to this pattern. Recently, however, the tree cover has been brought closer in on the outer sides of the south lawn to mask the airport bank. A vista has also been cut through the woodland to the south of the house.

Plan from the Survey by Thomas Addison, 1781

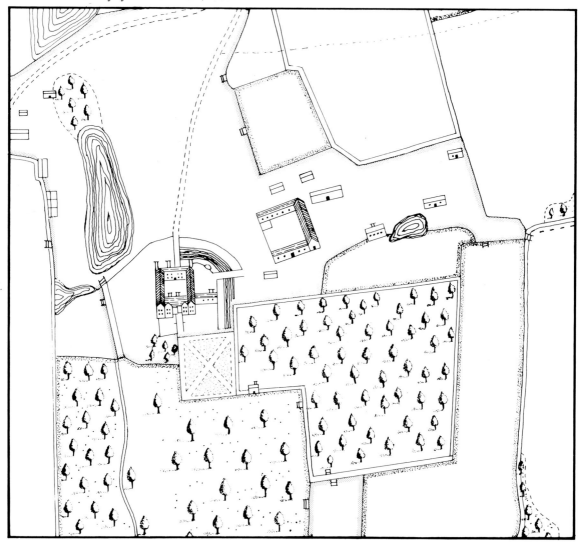

Plans of the House, with room names used in 1917

**Ground Floor**

**First Floor**

1   vestibule
2   lamp room
3   servants' hall
4   dairy
5   kitchen
6   scullery
7   vegetable larder
8   laundry
9   game larder
10  butler's pantry
11  beer cellar
12  wine cellar
13  housekeeper's room
14  blue drawing room
15  great hall
16  oak drawing room
17  cloakroom
18  gun room
19  library
20  billiard room
21  morning room

22  tapestry room
23  bathroom
24  bachelors room
25  no. 1 bedroom
26  housemaids' pantry
27  no. 2 bedroom
28  no. 3 bedroom
29  menservants' bedrooms
30  visitor's bedroom
31  courtyard bedroom
32  maids' bedroom
33  storerooms
34  nursery
35  inner bedroom
36  dressing room
37  St Raymond's room
38  maple room
39  dressing room
40  blue bedroom
41  dressing room
42  oak room
43  green bedroom
44  dressing room

# Acknowledgments

## Printed Sources

ANON
'Speke Hall', *Country Life*, 13/20 March 1903.

FARRER, W. AND BROWNBILL, J. (eds.)
*Victoria History of the Counties of England: Lancashire*, volume III, 1907.

HUSSEY, C.
'Speke Hall', *Country Life*, 7/14 January 1922.

NICHOLSON, S.
'Farming on a south Lancashire estate 1066–1795: evidence from Speke Hall', *Merseyside Archaeological Journal*, volume 3, 1983.

PEVSNER, N.
*Buildings of England: South Lancashire*, 1969.

SAXTON, E. B.
'Speke Hall and Two Norris Inventories, 1624 and 1700', *Transactions of the Historic Society of Lancashire and Cheshire*, volume 96 for 1944, 1945.

SAXTON, E. B.
'A Speke Inventory of 1624', *THSLC*, volume 97 for 1945, 1946.

WINSTANLEY, H.
'Speke Hall', *THSLC*, volume 79, 1919.

I am grateful to many friends and colleagues with whom I have discussed the history of Speke and this guidebook. In particular, Peter Locke and Carol Thickins, of Donald W Insall & Associates Ltd, the Consultant Architects, have endured endless conversations on the subject. The City Librarian and staff of the Liverpool Record Office have allowed full access to the Norris and Watt Papers and have provided every assistance.
Julian Gibbs, Belinda Cousens and Gervase Jackson-Stops of the National Trust read and made a number of useful comments on the text.

A.J.T.     August 1982

The plan from the Survey by Thomas Addison is reproduced by kind permission of Sykes Waterhouse & Co.

## Manuscript Sources

There are Norris Papers in the British Library, Liverpool University Library and the City Record Office, Liverpool City Libraries. Estate Papers for the late 19th and early 20th centuries are also in the City Record Office.
Abstracts from the Norris Papers are printed in Lumby, J. H., 'A Calendar of the Norris Deeds', *Lancashire and Cheshire Record Society*, volume 93, 1939, and Heywood, T., 'The Norris Papers', *Chetham Society*, 1846.

ISBN 0 906367 13 1

Set in Monophoto Photina by
August Filmsetting
Haydock, Merseyside

Printed by
Eaton Press Ltd.
Wallasey, Merseyside

Designed by Barrie Jones

Cover design by Neil Weir

British Library Cataloguing in Publication Data

Tibbles, Anthony
   Speke Hall
   1.Speke Hall (Liverpool, Merseyside)—
   Guide-books
   I.Title
   914.27'53     DA664.L8

ISBN 0-906367-13-1

Speke Hall is situated 8 miles south-east of Liverpool, off the A561, near to Liverpool Airport.

For further information contact
Speke Hall, The Walk, Liverpool L24 1XD
051-427 7231